TURTLES

ANITA BASKIN-SALZBERG & ALLEN SALZBERG

TURTLES

FRANKLIN WATTS
A Division of Grolier Publishing
New York / London / Hong Kong / Sydney
Danbury, Connecticut
A FIRST BOOK

To the people of the
New York Turtle and Tortoise Society,
in appreciation.

Frontispiece: A row of western painted turtles bask in the sun to get warm.

Cover photographs copyright ©: A. B. Sheldon (front cover: eastern box turtle);
Suzanne L. Collins & Joseph T. Collins (back cover: common map turtle).

Photographs copyright ©: A. B. Sheldon: pp. 2, 3; Animals Animals: pp. 8, 11, 12, 18, 27, 37
(all Zig Leszczynski), 14 (Robert A. Lubeck), 20, 38 (both Carlo Dani/Ingrid Jeske),
25 (Klaus Uhlenhut), 30 (Joe McDonald), 42 (David C. Fritts), 45 (Thomas Zuraw), 51
(C. C. Lockwood), Comstock: pp. 17, 34, 41, 47; Suzanne L. Collins & Joseph T. Collins:
p. 23; P. C. H. Pritchard: p. 32.

Library of Congress Cataloging-in-Publication Data

Baskin-Salzberg, Anita.
Turtles / Anita Baskin-Salzberg and Allen Salzberg.
p. cm. — (A First book)
Includes bibliographical references (p.   ) and index.
Summary: Describes different kinds of turtles, tortoises, and sea turtles
and the endangered status of some species.
ISBN 0-531-20220-8
1. Turtles—Juvenile literature. 2. Endangered species—Juvenile literature.
[1. Turtles. 2. Endangered species.] I. Salzberg, Allen. II. Title. III. Series.
QL666.C5819 1996
597.92—dc20
95-45362
CIP AC

CONTENTS

A TURTLE IS MORE THAN ITS SHELL

Most people think of turtles as slow-moving animals that carry their homes on their backs. A turtle, however, is much more than its shell.

The world's more than 250 turtle *species* are found on every continent except Antarctica and in every ocean except the Arctic. They live in rivers, lakes, oceans, forests, jungles, and deserts, and they even live underground.

The world's smallest turtles include the 3- to 3.5-inch (8- to 9-cm) eastern bog turtle and the 4- to 5-ounce (113- to 142-g) speckled cape and parrot-beaked *tortoises* of western and southern Africa.

The largest living turtles include: the

Three turtle hatchlings emerge from eggs.

Galápagos tortoise, which may weigh more than 500 pounds (227 kg); the alligator snapper, which can grow to over 300 pounds (136 kg); and the leatherback sea turtle, which can tip the scales at over 1 ton (907 kg).

Turtles live very long lives. Water turtles can outlive a cat or a dog, while some land turtles have lived to be over one hundred years old.

Many turtles move faster than people realize. A soft-shelled turtle can outswim trout, one of the fastest moving fish, and sea turtles have been clocked swimming at 15 miles (24 km) per hour.

All turtles are reptiles. Reptiles, which include snakes, lizards, crocodiles, and alligators, share many characteristics. Most reptiles lay eggs and have scaly skin. All reptiles use lungs to breathe. Unlike mammals or birds, reptiles depend on their environment for heat. Such animals are called *ectotherms*. What sets a turtle apart from all other reptiles is its shell.

THE FIRST TURTLES

Turtles first appeared about the same time as dinosaurs, during the Triassic period more than 200 million years ago. That was long before snakes, lizards, crocodiles, and alligators arrived on the scene. The thick, heavy shells of the first turtles could defeat the sharp teeth and claws of a variety of attackers.

One of the oldest known turtles, *Proganochelys*, was wider than it was long. Like other prehistoric turtles, it could not withdraw its neck into its shell. Judging from its large, strong limbs, it probably walked on land. The neck and tail of *Proganochelys* were covered with bony armor, which protected it against predators. Unlike today's turtles, *Proganochelys* had teeth.

With its 12-foot- (3.7-m-) long shell that may have weighed up to 2 to 3 tons (1,814 to 2,722 kg), the sea turtle *Archelon* was as big as a small car. Archelon lived in the Niobara Sea, which covered the central plains of the United States between what is now South Dakota and Texas during the upper Cretaceous period 100 million years ago.

A SHELL GAME

While dinosaurs have been extinct for a long time, turtles have survived, thanks to one of nature's most successful designs—the turtle shell. Unlike other animals with shells, such as armadillos, a turtle's shell is fused bone. A turtle's rib cage and spinal

*These young water turtles are called map turtles
after the maplike patterns on their shells.*

11

The lower and upper sections of a turtle's shell are attached with "bridges" of shell along both sides of the body.

cord are actually part of its shell. A turtle can never leave its shell, any more than a person can leave his or her skin.

The outside of the shell is covered by a layer of *keratin*, the same material that your fingernails are made of, which gives the shell its color. The keratin is divided into sections called *scutes*. The upper section of a turtle's shell is called the *carapace* (CARE-uh-pace). The lower section of the shell is called the *plastron*. The carapace and plastron are joined on the turtle's left and right sides by "bridges" of shell.

Turtle shells are wonderful protection. When a turtle is afraid of a predator or a person, it will pull its head, legs, and tail into its safe shell, out of reach of a predator's teeth and claws and protected from a person's grasp.

Some species of turtles are unable to hide completely in their shells and protect themselves from enemies in other ways. The musk turtle gives off a foul smell. The common snapping turtle and the soft-shelled turtle defend themselves with strong jaws and sharp claws. And a colorful shell can help a water turtle blend in with the plants and rocks along a shore.

The box turtle has a hinged plastron that it closes up like a trapdoor when threatened.

SCALY SKIN

The skin on a turtle's limbs is covered with rough scales, which helps prevent the body's moisture from evaporating, even in the desert. (Because they have no sweat glands, turtles can't sweat.) Scaly skin, especially if it is ridged, can also discourage predators.

BREATHING

If you put your hands on your chest and stomach, you will notice that both are flexible and move in and out as you breathe. For a turtle with its rigid shell, breathing is more complex. Inside the shell, a pair of muscles pulls a membrane behind the lungs forward to compress them and force the air out. Then these muscles relax and another pair of muscles pulls the membrane back against the turtle's abdominal organs and air is drawn into the lungs. Breathing is also assisted by movements of the turtle's limbs and pulsations of its throat.

Water turtles do not need as much oxygen as people do. They can stay under water for hours without coming up for air. Some water turtles can increase that time by absorbing oxygen directly from the water. When water is drawn into the turtle's *cloaca*, the anal opening under its tail, oxygen from the water passes through the lining of the cloaca into the turtle's bloodstream. The turtle may also absorb oxygen through tiny blood vessels in its throat.

When a turtle pulls itself into its shell, air comes out of the lungs to make room for its head and limbs. The hissing sound you hear when a turtle rapidly withdraws its head is this expulsion of air.

CATCHING AND EATING FOOD

Instead of teeth, turtles have sharp jaws with hard, sharp edges that cut. Tortoises are *herbivorous* and eat mostly plants. *Omnivorous* box turtles eat fruits, vegetables, worms, and other insects. *Carnivorous* water turtles eat mostly meat or fish.

Some turtles have unique ways of catching food. The matamata's head looks like a plant. When a small fish swims close to its head, the turtle quickly opens its mouth and expands its large neck, and the fish is sucked in as if into a vacuum cleaner. The turtle then spits out the water and swallows its prey whole.

Many water turtles, including loggerhead turtles, absorb oxygen from the water through an opening under the tail called a cloaca.

An eastern box turtle lays an egg into a freshly dug nest.

REPRODUCTION

Turtles reproduce by laying eggs. The female turtle digs a nest in the soil or sand with her hind legs and lays her eggs in the nest. She covers her eggs and departs. In a few months, the eggs hatch by themselves.

A hatchling turtle's life is full of danger. Big birds and small animals, like skunks, often make a meal out of a young turtle. Predators like raccoons and opossums also dig up turtle nests and eat the eggs.

Some scientists believe that only one in one hundred hatchling turtles lives to adulthood. Once a turtle becomes an adult, it has fewer enemies than it did as a hatchling.

Turtle, Tortoise, or Terrapin?

Turtles are called by different names in different parts of the English-speaking world.

	Land Turtle	Freshwater Turtle	Ocean-going Turtle
United States	Tortoise	Turtle	Sea Turtle
Great Britain	Tortoise	Terrapin	Turtle
Australia	Tortoise	Tortoise	Turtle

However, turtles' scientific names are the same all over the world. For example, the diamondback terrapin's scientific name is *Malaclemys terrapin*, and the common snapping turtle is called *Chelydra serpentina*.

The alligator snapping turtle uses a wormlike appendage on its tongue to lure small fish into its mouth.

FRESHWATER TURTLES

Over two-thirds of all turtle species live in freshwater—in rivers and ponds, lakes and streams, and even small rain puddles along the side of dirt roads. Freshwater turtles are found on six of the seven continents.

More than five turtle species can live in different parts of the same stretch of a freshwater river. Mud and musk turtles may crawl among algae-covered rocks in shallow water, searching for worms and other food. Common and alligator snapping turtles hide among fallen branches and tree roots near the shore. Painted and slider turtles live in the open water, basking on logs or rocks.

THE FRESHWATER TURTLE'S SHELL

The shells of water turtles are much flatter than the shells of tortoises. A flat shell helps water turtles cut through the water efficiently, in much the same way an airplane wing cuts through the air. Not all water turtle shells are exactly alike. A loggerhead musk turtle's shell, for example, is domed in the front to allow it to retract its large head partially into its shell.

The soft-shelled turtle has the flattest shell of all freshwater turtles. Its flat shell helps to make it a very fast swimmer. Its shell also acts like the blade of a shovel, helping the turtle to dig beneath the sand, its favorite hiding place.

Once they are hidden in the muddy bottom of a lake or stream, soft-shelled turtles wait patiently for a fish or another animal to come within striking range. Then, moving like a jack-in-the-box, the turtle shoots out its exceptionally long neck and grabs its prey.

In the winter, many water turtles that live in cold climates bury themselves in the mud beneath the water. Then they go into a deep sleep called hibernation that lasts until spring.

WEBBED FEET

All freshwater turtles have webbed feet, with folds of skin between each claw. The webbing helps the tur-

The unique, leathery shells of soft-shelled turtles, like this spiny softshell, have no scutes.

tle displace more water with each stroke of its legs, pushing it forward in the water longer and faster.

Generally speaking, the more aquatic the turtle, the more webbing it has between its claws. *Semiaquatic* North American wood turtles spend a portion of their lives in water. These turtles have almost no webbing between their claws. However, the foot of a soft-shelled turtle, which lives in the water almost all the time, is almost completely webbed.

HIDDEN-NECKED AND SIDE-NECKED TURTLES

Scientists divide all turtles into two suborders. Their scientific names are *Cryptodira* (hidden-necked turtles) and *Pleurodira* (side-necked turtles).

All North American turtles and tortoises are hidden-necked turtles. They draw their necks into an **S** curve as they pull their heads into their shells.

All side-necked turtles are aquatic turtles. About fifty species of side-necked turtles live south of the equator. Very few species live in tropical regions north of the equator. To withdraw its head, a side-necked turtle folds its neck sideways underneath its carapace.

An interesting family of side-necked turtles are the snake-necked turtles of Australia, New Guinea,

The Northern Australian snake-necked turtle can stretch its neck longer than 75 percent of its roughly 14-inch (35-cm) carapace.

and South America. The necks of these turtles are as long as, and sometimes longer than, their shells and move like a snake. Snake-necked turtles use their long necks to reach prey that hides between rocks and logs. Like soft-shelled turtles, these turtles use their long necks to strike out quickly and catch fish.

TERRAPINS AND BOX TURTLES

Although related to freshwater turtles, diamondback terrapins and North American box turtles don't live in freshwater. Diamondback terrapins may look like typical freshwater turtles, but they live in the partly salty, or brackish, waters of marshes and river inlets along the coastline of the eastern United States from Massachusetts to Texas.

Although they are descended from freshwater turtles, most box turtles are land turtles with domed shells like tortoises. However, one box turtle species prefers water to land—the Coahuilan box turtle of Mexico, which lives in shallow bodies of water.

Diamondback terrapins are carnivorous and eat snails, crabs, aquatic worms, and insects.

Common Species of North American Water Turtles

Turtle and Habitat	Physical Characteristics	Unusual Facts
Common Musk Turtle From New England and Ontario, Canada, to Florida to Wisconsin to Texas. Lives in waterways with soft bottoms and slow currents: rivers, ponds, and swamps.	Grows to 5 inches (13 cm). Has a black carapace, a small plastron, and three distinctive yellow stripes on each side of its head.	Emits a foul odor to discourage predators. In the wild, its shell may be covered with algae.
Common Snapping Turtle From Nova Scotia, Canada, to Florida to all areas east of the Rocky Mountains. Prefers river and lake bottoms.	Two U.S. subspecies and two Central and South American subspecies. Can grow to 18 inches (46 cm), excluding neck and tail. Has a tan to black carapace, sharp jaws, and long, heavily serrated tail.	It is known as a vicious turtle, but there are no records of unprovoked attacks on people. Scavengers, they eat everything from aquatic plants to dead fish.
Map Turtle Southern United States, especially the Mississippi River drainage systems and Texas. Prefers clear rivers or streams with basking sites, such as fallen trees.	Eleven species and several subspecies. Grows to between 7 and 13 inches (18 and 33 cm). The carapace, limbs, head, and tail are colored with patterns that resemble a road map.	Some species, like the sawbacks, have high ridges on the carapace. Many species are threatened by industrial pollution and development along their river homes.
Painted Turtle As far north as Nova Scotia, Canada, as far south as Georgia, and as far west as Colorado. Lives in slow-moving shallow water, including ponds and lakes.	Four subspecies. Grows to between 6 and 10 inches (15 and 25 cm). Has olive-brown shell with yellow, orange, and red stripes on legs, neck, and head.	Northern hatchlings have a natural form of "anti-freeze" in their blood that helps them survive buried underground in subfreezing temperatures. They lose this ability with age.
Slider Turtle From southeast Virginia to northern Florida, west to Kansas and New Mexico, and throughout Central and South America as far south as Brazil.	At least fourteen subspecies. Grows to between 8 and 24 inches (20 and 60 cm). Hatchlings' green, yellow, and black markings cover the carapace but fade with age.	Males are smaller than females, and some have long front claws that they wave in front of females during courtship. Over 15 million red-eared slider hatchlings were sold yearly as pets until their sale was banned in 1975.
Soft-Shelled Turtle Throughout the United States, except the Northeast. Prefers soft muddy-bottomed rivers, with sandbars for nesting.	Three species: smooth, spiny, and Florida softshells. The largest species, the Florida softshell, grows to 2 feet (61 cm).	Has a flattened carapace, long neck, and long snoutlike nose. Males are often less than half the size of full-grown females.

28

TORTOISES

Turtles that have adapted specially to live on land are called tortoises. Most of the nearly fifty species of tortoises live in hot, dry regions in the southern parts of the world.

The smallest tortoise is the speckled cape tortoise of southern Africa, which grows to only 4 inches (10 cm) long. The largest tortoises live on the Galápagos Islands, off the coast of Ecuador. They grow, on average, to 3 to 4 feet (91 to 122 cm) long and can weigh over 500 pounds (227 kg).

Tortoises move very slowly. It can take some tortoises five hours to walk one mile. A tortoise's elephantlike hind feet are perfectly suited for walk-

The Galápagos tortoise is one of the largest land turtles.
European explorers stored these tortoises alive in the holds
of their ships as a food source during the long voyage home.

ing on land. Tortoises have only four toes on each foot and thick, heavy scales on their front limbs. When in danger, they use their front legs as a shield to cover their faces.

Tortoises that live in the desert may spend as much as six months underground hibernating during the winter. Some tortoises, like Russian or Horsfield's tortoises from Russia, Iran, Afghanistan, and Pakistan not only hibernate in winter, but spend long periods of time underground, out of the hot summer sun. This is called estivation.

A typical tortoise starts the day at sunrise, warming itself and foraging for food. By midday, it has moved into the shade of grass, bushes, or tall rocks. In late afternoon, a tortoise becomes active again and spends the night in its burrow. Tortoises live long lives and may take ten to fifteen years to reach breeding age.

SHELL COLOR

The shells of most tortoises are shades of tan, brown, and black to help them blend with the earth, sand, rocks, and grass of their habitats. Some tortoises, including Madagascar's radiated tortoise, South Africa's geometric tortoise, and Asia's Indian

The geometric tortoise, which lives in South Africa, is one of the world's rarest turtles.

star tortoise, have shells covered with beautiful black and brown or yellow star-burst patterns. These markings help the turtles conceal themselves in full view in their grassland homes, especially during the early morning or late afternoon when the sun produces the strongest shadows.

Although radiated, geometric, and star tortoises are found in different countries, their shells look alike. This is an example of *convergent evolution*, which occurs when unrelated animals that live in similar habitats develop similar survival adaptations.

SOME INTERESTING TORTOISE SPECIES

AFRICAN HINGE-BACK TORTOISE The African hinge-back tortoise is the only turtle with a hinge on its carapace, not on its plastron. The hinge enables the turtle to close off the rear of its shell. There are four species of hingebacks. Unlike other tortoises, two hinge-back species—the Home's and serrated—live in moist areas and are omnivorous. The serrated hingeback, a fair swimmer, is known to hunt tadpoles and small fish.

Two giant Aldabra tortoises forage on Aldabra Island.

GIANT TORTOISE The world's largest tortoises live on tropical islands in the Indian and Pacific Oceans. Many species of giant tortoises are in danger of extinction. Predators introduced by humans, including goats, dogs, cats, and rats, prey on tortoise eggs and hatchlings and threaten the survival of some giant tortoises.

There are few predators on Aldabra Island, off the east coast of Africa. As a result, the population of Aldabra tortoises, with over one hundred thousand tortoises, has grown very large, but that is an unusual case.

GOPHER TORTOISE The gopher tortoise of the southeastern United States inhabits sandy-soiled, broad-leafed woodland and grassland. This tortoise's powerful front limbs and strong claws help it dig a burrow up to 30 feet (9 m) long to live in all year round. Snakes, mice, rabbits, lizards, frogs, toads, and as many as forty different species of insects and spiders share the burrow with the tortoise.

The burrows' stable temperature and humidity allow the tortoises to remain active underground during the hottest part of the day. They emerge at night to forage for a dinner of grass, leaves, fruit, insects, and water.

PANCAKE TORTOISE The African pancake tortoise lives in the arid scrub and thornbush thickets of Kenya and Tanzania. Its thin, pliable shell is flat like a pancake. To escape a predator, the pancake tortoise will wedge itself between two flat rocks, where no enemy can reach it.

FIGHTING OVER FEMALES

Tortoises are peaceful creatures until mating time, when the males battle for the chance to mate with a female. They bite each other's necks and ram their shells into each other, fighting like miniature tanks. A male plowshare tortoise from Madagascar uses his long *gular* (GOO-lar) scute, a projection on the front of the plastron just under the head, to flip a rival on his back.

Tortoises can emit a variety of noises during courtship and mating. South American yellow-footed tortoises make clucking sounds, giant Aldabra tortoises bellow, African spur-thighed tortoises give short grunts and groans, and hinge-back tortoises hiss.

Male tortoises fight until one retreats, or is flipped over on his back. If the loser is unable to right himself, his shell can become a tomb, trapping the turtle in the sun and roasting it alive.

The flat pancake tortoise, also called the crevice tortoise, lives with spiders, snakes, and scorpions in narrow openings between rocks.

37

A ferocious fighter, the plowshare tortoise can overturn an opponent using his gular scute, a projection under the head.

Some Tortoises of the World

Tortoise and Habitat	Physical Characteristics	Unusual Facts
Asian Brown Tortoise Highland monsoon forests of India, Bangladesh, Myanmar, Thailand, Malaysia, Sumatra, and Borneo.	The largest Asian land tortoise, with a brown carapace of up to 2 feet (61 cm).	Almost totally dark brown to black in color. Burrows into moist soil or under leaves. Builds large mound of leaves over its nest.
Desert Tortoise Southwestern United States. Lives in desert oases, canyon bottoms, and sandy or rocky soil.	Grows to between 6 and 14 inches (15 and 35 cm). Its brownish shell has lighter colored spots on each scute.	Lives in 33-foot- (10-m-) long burrows. Digs in dry, gravely soil under bushes. Several tortoises may use the same burrow.
Galápagos Tortoise Volcanic Galápagos Islands, off the coast of Ecuador.	Grows to between 2.6 and 4 feet (80 and 120 cm). Can weigh more than 500 pounds (227 kg).	Twelve species in existence. They may have reached the islands on natural vegetative debris blown by storms from the mainland.
Hermann's Tortoise The Mediterranean Sea from Spain to the Balkans to Turkey.	Can grow to 8 inches (20 cm). Has a yellowish cream, rounded carapace with dark brown markings.	Usually forages for food late at night. Hundreds of thousands of Hermann's tortoises were once shipped to Europe from Yugoslavia as pets.
Leopard Tortoise Almost every African country south of the Sahara Desert. Lives in grasslands and plains.	Can grow to 27 inches (69 cm). Young are marked with leopardlike spots on a cream-colored shell. The shell fades to tan or brown with age.	Lays from 5 to 30 eggs, which may incubate for over a year. Eats succulent plants and grasses.
Padloper Tortoise (or **speckled cape tortoise** of South Africa) Prefers arid woodland or grassland.	Grows to 4 inches (10 cm). Is cream to yellowish green colored, with black spots or radiations.	The world's smallest turtle. Courtship consists of rhythmic sweeps of the head. Lays one egg per clutch (nest) that is over one-third the turtle's size.
South American Red-Footed Tortoise Colombia, Venezuela, Brazil, Bolivia, Paraguay, and Argentina. Lives in moist grasslands.	Grows to 20 inches (51 cm). Has a black carapace and front legs with brilliant red markings.	Males identify females by smell and other males by responsive head movements.

SEA TURTLES

Sea turtles are some of the largest turtles in the world and live in almost every ocean of the world. Their smooth shells and paddlelike flippers help them speed through the water as fast as 15 miles (24 km) per hour. These long-distance travelers have been known to swim up to 3,000 miles (4,828 km).

Although sea turtles cannot withdraw their heads into their shells, the adults are protected from predators by their shells, large size, and thick scaly skin on their heads and necks.

Because sea turtles are difficult to study in the open ocean, scientists are just beginning to learn about the life history of sea turtles. Today, radio

*Like their smaller freshwater cousins, sea turtles
have strong jaws, but no teeth. Most marine turtles
eat sea grasses or crabs and other crustaceans.*

41

Sea turtle eggs hatch within the nest at nearly the same time. Over the following two to three days, only the strongest and fastest hatchlings, thrashing their way up through the nest and to the sea, survive.

transmitters, attached to nesting turtles, help track the sea creatures on their travels and provide valuable information.

NESTING

Although sea turtles move swiftly in the ocean, they are slow and defenseless on land. Male sea turtles almost never leave the water. Female sea turtles leave the ocean only to lay eggs and, for most species, nest only at night. A female may nest every two to three years.

Nesting can take between one and three hours. After a female turtle drags herself up the beach, she hollows out a pit with her back legs and deposits from fifty to two hundred eggs the size of golf balls. When the last egg is laid, the turtle covers the eggs with sand, tamps down the sand with her plastron, and flings more sand about with her flippers to erase any signs of the nest.

After about two months, the hatchling turtles emerge at night. The light reflected off the water from the sky guides them to the sea. These days, car headlights, street lamps, or lights on buildings near the beach cause some hatchlings to travel in the wrong direction. Waiting herons make fast meals of other hatchlings. Any babies still on the beach in the morning are easily picked off by predators or die in the hot sun. It is thought that when the surviving hatchlings reach maturity, they return to the beach where they hatched to lay their eggs.

THE SEVEN SEA TURTLE SPECIES

AUSTRALIAN FLATBACK This medium-sized sea turtle nests on beaches in unpopulated areas of the northern coast of Australia. Saltwater crocodiles, as well as monitor lizards and foxes, sometimes eat small adult turtles while they are nesting.

GREEN This medium-to-large sea turtle gets its name from the green color of its body fat. Its smooth olive-brown carapace is heart shaped. Its serrated beak, notched like the edge of a saw, helps it feed on turtle grass and other marine plants. Green sea turtles in the eastern Pacific Ocean are called black sea turtles, although some scientists consider the black sea turtle a separate species.

HAWKSBILL This medium-sized sea turtle with a shield-shaped shell is found in tropical waters around the world. Named for its birdlike beak, the hawksbill usually nests near its feeding grounds and

The beautiful hawksbill has been hunted for centuries for its multicolored "tortoiseshell" scutes.

mates in shallow water off the nesting beach. Hawksbills climb over reefs and rocks to nest among the roots of vegetation on beaches.

KEMP'S RIDLEY Also called the Atlantic ridley, the Kemp's ridley is the world's most endangered sea turtle. Very little is known of its habits. It is known that between April and mid-August, the turtles nest in large groups called *arribadas*, Spanish for "arrival," in only one place in the world: a beach near Rancho Nuevo, Mexico. In 1947, over forty thousand female Kemp's ridley turtles nested on that beach in a single day; in 1992, only five hundred came to nest.

LEATHERBACK The largest of all sea turtles, the leatherback can grow to over 7 feet (2 m) long. These tireless swimmers have been found throughout the world's oceans, as far north as Newfoundland and as far south as the southern coast of Chile. Leatherbacks can also dive to great depths, as far as 3,000 feet (914 m) deep, probably in search of their favorite food—jellyfish.

LOGGERHEAD Known for its massive reddish brown head, the large omnivorous loggerhead sea turtle eats fish, jellyfish, mussels, clams, squid,

The most abundant of sea turtles, olive ridleys have flattened, broad carapaces and nest at night.

shrimp, seaweed, and marine grasses. The logger-head travels widely and has been found as far as 500 miles (805 km) offshore. In many areas of the world, this turtle is hunted for its meat and eggs.

OLIVE RIDLEY Also called the Pacific ridley, this small sea turtle has paddlelike flippers and grows up to 28 inches (71 cm) long. A speedy nester, it spends only about forty-five minutes on the beach laying its eggs. Like the Kemp's ridley, it nests in *arribadas*.

Sea Turtles of the World

Turtle and Habitat	Physical Characteristics	Unusual Facts
Australian Flatback Sea Turtle Northern Australia.	Grows to between 36 and 39 inches (91 and 99 cm). Weighs about 160 pounds (73 kg). Has a flat carapace and olive-gray scutes.	Lays about 50 large eggs, 2 inches (5 cm) in diameter. An early evening nester.
Green Sea Turtle Parts of the Atlantic, Pacific, and Indian Oceans, mostly in the tropics.	Heart-shaped shell 4 feet (120 cm) long. Weighs an average of 300 pounds (136 kg).	Herbivorous. Grazes on sea grasses and algae. Nests on beaches in Costa Rica, South America, and sometimes on the Atlantic coast of Florida.
Hawksbill Sea Turtle Tropical waters worldwide, especially near coral reefs and shallow coastal waters.	A small turtle that grows to between 30 and 35 inches (76 and 89 cm) and 100 and 250 pounds (45 and 114 kg).	Its black and yellow scutes are sought for tortoiseshell jewelry. A solitary nester, it lays between 70 and 150 eggs.
Kemp's Ridley Sea Turtle Atlantic Ocean from Central America to Nova Scotia, Canada.	Grows to between 22 and 27 inches (56 and 69 cm). Weighs between 85 and 100 pounds (39 and 45 kg). Has a flattened, broad carapace and massive jaws.	Lives in shallow coastal waters of 150 feet (46 m) or less. The most endangered sea turtle. Nests by day.
Leatherback Sea Turtle Atlantic, Pacific, and Indian Oceans. As far north as Labrador, Canada, as far south as Chile.	The largest sea turtle. Grows to 74 inches (1.9 m). Can weigh between 700 pounds and 1 ton (318 and 907 kg).	Its carapace lacks scutes. Can dive to great depths. Its throat is lined with backward-pointing spines, which help it ingest slippery jellyfish.
Loggerhead Sea Turtle Subtropics worldwide.	Large, reddish brown shell. Grows to between 36 and 40 inches (91 and 102 cm) and 250 and 350 pounds (114 and 159 kg).	May nest as many as seven times between April and October. Lays from 64 to 200 eggs.
Olive Ridley Sea Turtle Tropical waters of the Pacific, Atlantic, and Indian Oceans.	One of the smallest sea turtles. Its shell length is about 25 inches (63 cm) and it weighs between 80 and 100 pounds (36 and 45 kg).	The most abundant sea turtle. Nests by night in large groups.

TURTLES
IN TROUBLE

Today, almost half of all turtle species are in trouble. Some species are at risk of becoming extinct within ten years, and over a hundred more may be extinct within fifty years.

There are five main reasons why turtles become extinct:

1. HABITAT DESTRUCTION When people clear forests, wetlands, and land near beaches to build hotels, houses, and highways, they rob turtles of places to live and lay eggs.

The Southeast Asian spiny turtle, for example, thrives in teak and mahogany forests. When

To prevent sea turtles from drowning in shrimping nets, shrimpers must fit their nets with TEDs, or turtle extruder devices. However, other nets, like driftnets, are still a menace to turtles, such as this loggerhead.

those rain forests are harvested for wood, seasonal downpours wash topsoil into rivers and streams, clouding them and killing the plants and animals the turtles feed on.

2. HUNTING Since ancient times, sea turtles have been hunted for their meat, oil, eggs, and scutes.

If the demand for turtle meat and products is confined to local peoples, relatively few turtles are usually killed. For example, although native peoples still eat large Southeast Asian and South American river turtles, as long as they kill only the turtles they wish to eat, river turtle populations as a whole are not harmed. However, many turtle species are at risk of extinction due to commercial hunting—hunting an animal not for individual use, but for sale.

As transportation has become faster and cheaper, making shipping to distant parts of the globe easy, the market for turtle products has become worldwide. Today, turtle skin is used to make belts and boots, turtle meat is a soup ingredient, and turtle shells are made into such souvenirs as tortoiseshell combs and eyeglasses or ground into powder for some Asian herbal medicines. Sea turtle eggs are even sold as aphrodisiacs, substances said to increase sexual desire.

3. PREDATORS Animals from rats to raccoons eat turtle eggs or hatchling turtles.

In the southwestern United States, scavengers such as ravens have flourished due to the expanding number of landfills. Not only do ravens feed on baby desert tortoises, but they kill and eat young tortoises with their long beaks.

4. ENVIRONMENTAL POLLUTION Air and water pollution kill turtles or the food they live on.

Recently banned, long-lived chemicals like DDT and PCBs still pollute the muddy bottoms of many U.S. rivers and lakes. Because snapping turtles hide and dig for food in the mud, snappers from New York's Hudson River and the Great Lakes have been found to have high levels of these deadly chemicals in their bodies. Scientists believe it may explain the recent decrease in snapping turtle eggs and increase in deformed snapping turtle hatchlings throughout the Great Lakes region.

5. ALIEN SPECIES AND DISEASES Each year, thousands of U.S. slider turtles are sold overseas as pets. Hardy red-eared sliders are breeding in South Africa, pushing out the native turtle populations. They are also found in rivers in Italy and southern France, where they compete for food with smaller native European pond turtles.

Pet turtles can also introduce diseases to wild populations. In the 1950s and 1960s, many Californians released pet desert tortoises back into the

53

desert. Those pet turtles spread a lethal respiratory disease to their wild counterparts.

Some turtle populations, filled with adults, may seem healthy and thriving. The adults, however, are often old, and the young turtles are threatened by pollution, predators, and overdevelopment. If no young survive to replace the adults, the turtle population eventually disappears.

Five of the World's Most Endangered Turtles

Turtle and Habitat	Physical Characteristics	Threats to Survival
Abingdon Island Tortoise Galápagos Islands, off the coast of Ecuador.	Grows to 39 inches (98 cm). The front of its black carapace is shaped like the front of a horse's saddle.	There is only one known living adult of this species. Lonesome George resides at the Charles Darwin Station on Indefatigable Island.
Geometric Tortoise South Africa.	Grows to 9 inches (24 cm). Has a dark brown carapace. Each scute has a yellow spot and stripes radiating outward.	These tortoises live in uncultivated areas prone to brush fires, capable of wiping an adult population out entirely.
Kemp's Ridley Sea Turtle Atlantic Ocean from Central America to Nova Scotia, Canada.	Has a yellow to gray carapace. Males have a claw on their forelimbs to hold onto females during mating.	Probably fewer than 600 adult females left in the world. These sea turtles are severely threatened by incidental capture in shrimp nets.
Plowshare Tortoise Dense forests of Northern Madagascar, off the southeastern coast of Africa.	Can grow to 1.5 feet (45 cm). Its gular (the extension on the front of the plastron) is so long, the turtle can rest its head on it.	Only 400 left in the wild. Development of its habitat and predation of its young by wild pigs endangers these tortoises.
Western Swamp Turtle Swamps outside Perth, Australia.	A 6-inch- (15-cm-) long side-necked turtle. Feeds on aquatic insects, crustaceans, and tadpoles.	Fewer than 150 in existence. First captive-raised babies were born in the early 1990s. Development threatens its habitat and survival.

HELP IS ON THE WAY

Despite the considerable obstacles that today's turtle populations face, their future is not entirely bleak. In the United States, federal laws have been passed to protect various endangered species, including bog turtles and desert tortoises, and their habitats. State laws are also in effect to protect locally endangered species such as gopher tortoises and wood turtles.

Over 120 countries signed the Convention on International Trade in Endangered Species (CITES), a treaty designed to monitor and control international trade in animals and plants. The agreements made by the member countries protect all sea turtles, tortoises, North American box turtles, and several species of freshwater turtles from overexploitation by the international wildlife trade.

Through research, education, and active participation, scientists, conservationists, and turtle lovers are working to save turtle populations all over the world.

GLOSSARY

Arribadas—Spanish for "arrival." It refers to large congregations of nesting turtles.

Carapace—The upper section of a turtle's shell.

Carnivorous—Describes an animal that feeds on other animals or animal matter.

Cloaca—The anal opening under a turtle's tail.

Convergent evolution—When unrelated animals living in similar habitats develop similar adaptations.

Cryptodira—The classification, or suborder, of turtles that can pull their necks directly back into their shells.

Ectotherm—An animal whose body temperature is dependent on the outside temperature.

Gular—The front scute or scutes of the plastron. In some tortoises, it projects out under the head.

Herbivorous—Describes an animal that feeds on plants.

Keratin—A protein substance that is the chief structural building-block of hair, nails, horns, hoofs, and turtle scutes.

Omnivorous—Describes an animal that feeds on plants and other animals.

Plastron—The lower section of a turtle's shell.

Pleurodira—The classification, or suborder, of turtles that can retract their neck sideways, underneath their carapace.

Scutes—The small, individual shields made of keratin that cover the outside of most turtle shells.

Semiaquatic—Adapted to live in both land and water.

Species—Related organisms capable of interbreeding.

Terrapin—In the United States, it refers to aquatic turtles, especially the diamondback terrapin. In Great Britain, it refers to all freshwater turtles.

Tortoise—Turtles that have adapted to living on land.

What You Can Do To Help Turtles

1. Leave turtles in the wild. Don't collect them as pets.

2. Help turtles cross the road. Place them on the side they were heading toward. Always be aware of passing traffic!

3. Carry injured turtles to a wildlife rehabilitator in a dark container with a clean, moistened towel.

4. Don't buy hatchling turtles as pets. It is illegal to buy or sell any turtles under 4 inches (10 cm) long in the United States. Hatchling (and adult turtles) can also carry salmonella, a kind of bacteria that causes a form of food poisoning.

5. Don't buy products made from turtles. Buy artificial tortoiseshell made from plastic, or mock turtle soup made of mushrooms instead of turtle meat.

FOR MORE INFORMATION ON HELPING TURTLES

THE NEW YORK TURTLE AND TORTOISE SOCIETY
>   163 Amsterdam Avenue
>   Suite 365
>   New York, NY 10023
>   *Send a self-addressed, stamped envelope for information on their turtle poster contest and free book list.*

CENTER FOR MARINE CONSERVATION
>   1725 DeSales Street NW
>   Suite 500
>   Washington, DC 20036
>   *Specializes in helping sea turtles.*

TURTLE RECOVERY PROGRAM
>   Wildlife Conservation Society
>   185th Street and Southern Blvd.
>   Bronx, NY 10460
>   *Sponsors scientific studies and plans conservation programs to help turtles and tortoises all over the world.*

WILDLIFE AND HABITAT PROTECTION PROGRAM
>   Humane Society of the United States
>   2100 L Street, NW
>   Washington, DC 20037
>   *Helps the effort to control the international trade in fresh-water turtles and tortoises.*

FOR FURTHER
READING

Ancona, George. *Turtle Watch*. New York: Macmillan Children's
    Books, 1987.

Arnold, Caroline. *Sea Turtles*. New York: Scholastic, Inc., 1994.

de Vosjoli, Philippe. *The General Care and Maintenance of Red-
    Eared Sliders and Other Popular Freshwater Turtles*.
    Lakeside, Calif.: Advanced Vivarium Systems, 1992.

de Vosjoli, Philippe, and Roger Klingenberg, D.V.M. *The Box
    Turtle Manual*. Lakeside, Calif.: Advanced Vivarium
    Systems, 1995.

Holling, Holling C. *Minn of the Mississippi*. Boston: Houghton
    Mifflin Co., 1992.

Schafer, Susan. *The Galápagos Tortoise*. New York: Dillon
    Press, Inc., 1992.

Wilke, Hartmut. *Turtles: A Complete Pet Owner's Manual*.
    Hauppauge, N.Y.: Barron's Educational Services, Inc.,
    1991.

Ziter, Cary B. *When Turtles Come to Town*. New York: Frank-
    lin Watts, 1989.

FOR REFERENCE ONLY

Ernst, Carl H., and Roger W. Barbour. *Turtles of the World*.
    Washington, D.C.: Smithsonian Institution Press, 1994.

Ernst, Carl H., Jeffrey E. Lovich, and Roger W. Barbour. *Turtles
    of the United States and Canada*. Washington, D.C.:
    Smithsonian Institution Press, 1994.

INDEX

ABOUT THE
AUTHORS

Turtles is the third Franklin Watts book for the Salzberg husband and wife team. Their last book, *Flightless Birds*, was named to the Science Books & Films Best Children's Science Book List in 1994.

Anita Baskin-Salzberg holds a master's degree in teaching from Northwestern University and works as a freelance copywriter and journalist. Allen Salzberg is an environmental marketer. He is also a member of the board of the New York Turtle and Tortoise Society.

The Salzbergs have written for *Ranger Rick*, *Omni*, *Health*, *Outside*, *E: The Environmental Magazine*, and the *New York Times Magazine*.

The Salzbergs live in Forest Hills, New York.